Growing Wildflowers

WRITER
HAZEL WHITE

PHOTOGRAPHER
SAXON HOLT

LAWN & GARDEN

Product Manager: CYNTHIA FOLLAND, NK LAWN & GARDEN CO.

Acquisition, Development and Production Services:
JENNINGS & KEEFE: Media Development, Corte Madera, CA

Acquisition: JACK JENNINGS, BOB DOLEZAL

Series Concept: BOB DOLEZAL

Project Director: JILL FOX

Developmental Editor: JILL FOX

Horticultural Consultant: RG TURNER JR

Photographic Director: SAXON HOLT

Art Director (interior): BRAD GREENE

Cover Designer: KAREN EMERSON

Page Make-up: BRAD GREENE

Copy Editor: VIRGINIA RICH

Proofreader: LYNN FERAR

Indexer: SYLVIA COATES

Photo Assistant: PEGGY HENRY

Additional Photographers: Page 17 (Dutchman's breeches)
and page 51 (Canada lily and Turk's cap lily) New England
Wildflower Society; page 51 (Wood lily) Charles Cresson;
page 51 (Michigan lily) John Harrington; page 53 (Texas
lupine) and pages 64-65 Charles Mann

Color Separations: PREPRESS ASSEMBLY INCORPORATED

Printing and Binding: WOLFER PRINTING COMPANY

PRINTED IN THE USA

Cover: Sun-loving blanket flower (see page 14), foreground,
and black-eyed Susan (see page 12) provide beautiful fall color
along a secluded garden path.

Public Gardens Photographed: Chanticleer, Wayne, PA;
Longwood Gardens, Kennet, Square, PA; Gardens-in-the-
Woods, Framingham, MA; Lindsey Museum, Walnut Creek,
CA; The Mount Cuba Center for the Study of Piedmont Flora,
Wilmingham, DE; University of California Botanic Garden,
Berkeley, CA; Strybing Arboretum, San Francisco, CA

First Edition

Library of Congress Cataloging-in-Publication Data:
White, Hazel.
    Growing wild flowers / writer, Hazel White ; photo-
grapher, Saxon Holt.
      p. cm.
    Includes index.
    ISBN 1-880281-15-5
    1. Wild flower gardening--United States. 2. Natural
landscaping--United States. 3. Wild flowers--United
States--Identification. 4. Wild flower gardening--Canada.
5. Natural landscaping--Canada. 6. Wild flowers-
Canada--Identification. I. Holt Saxon. II. Title.
    SB439.W48 1994
    635.9' 676'0973 --dc20   93-20811
                                                          CIP

Special thanks to: Annette Alexander; Dave Alosi; Valerie
Brown; Theo Crawford; Phil Edinger; Ross Edwards; Roger
Gettig; Ben Haggard; Gail Haggard, Plants of the Southwest,
Santa Fe, NM; Debbie Harwell; Peggy Henry; Larner Seeds,
Bolinas, CA; Dr. Richard Lighty, The Mount Cuba Center for
the Study of Piedmont Flora; McAllister's Water Gardens,
Napa, CA; Sandy Maillard; Cliff Miller; Laurie Otto; Robin
Parer; Liz Parsons; Barbara Pryor, The New England Wild-
flower Society; Janet Sanchez; Sara Shopkow; Steven Still;
Ray Sweet; Freeland Tanner; Katie Trefethen

95   96   97   10   9   8   7   6   5   4   3   2   1

TABLE OF CONTENTS

ENJOYING WILDFLOWERS

USING THIS BOOK

Consider this volume as three gardening books in one. The first is a guide to identifying popular wildflowers that are available to the home gardener. All the wildflowers in this book are reliable plants for gardens. The plants are presented alphabetically by common name, followed by the botanical name to help you find the right plant—many quite different plants share the same common name, but each has a unique botanical name.

Each wildflower is pictured and described so that you can quickly choose the best ones for your garden. Descriptions include each plant's blooming period; growing needs, whether it is easy to grow from seed or transplant; whether the plant attracts birds, bees and butterflies; and its viability for indoor arrangements. Turn to the Wildflower Reference Chart on page 74 for a quick referral.

The second book is a design manual. Panels of text and example photographs describe the basic principles of garden design and give the specifics for planning regional garden styles. Descriptions and lists of appropriate flowers for coastal, wetland, desert, rock, prairie and woodland gardens help you to duplicate these popular looks in any size yard.

Finally, this is a how-to garden book, with plenty of step-by-step information to get even the most novice gardener on the road to creating a beautiful wildflower garden. Pieces on preparing the soil, choosing plants, starting seeds, growing plants and year-round garden care provide a solid start to growing wildflowers. Use the index to find specific topics (see page 78).

Growing wildflowers in the garden is fun and easy. Use this book to plant a few flowers into an existing garden or recreate a natural habitat for birds, bees, butterflies and humans to enjoy.

What Is a Wildflower?

The wildflowers in this book are common North American natives. They are deemed "wildflowers" because of their beauty, but like the less attractive "weeds" that grow alongside them in the wild, they have a tremendous ability to survive.

While each region of the country has its own indigenous flowers, numerous ones, including most of the wildflowers in this book, are extremely adaptable. They have settled, or *naturalized,* far beyond their native range, are sold as seed or young plants in garden centers, nurseries and from catalogs and thrive in gardens. The United States Department of Agriculture has defined growing zones for each area of the country. Verify your USDA growing zone with a local nursery or county extension service agent. Check the Wildflower Reference Chart for the zones in which each plant will thrive (see page 74).

Wildflowers are either *annuals, perennials* or *biennials.* Annuals complete their life cycle within a year—the seed germinates in spring, the plant grows and flowers, insects or butterflies or bees pollinate the flowers, the seeds disperse in the wind and the plant dies in late fall. Some annuals reseed, or self-sow, readily. Perennials flower and set seed yearly. The evergreen ones keep their leaves all year. All perennial roots survive and push up new foliage in spring. Biennials complete their life cycle within two years, establishing a good root and foliage system in the first year and flowering, setting seed and dying in the second year.

Many nurseries sell cultivated varieties, or *cultivars,* of wildflowers, which have been bred by plant breeders. They are often showier than their wildflower parents, but sometimes less adaptable. Because so much native habitat is disappearing, always ask a nursery about the source of its wildflowers—to be sure the plant was commercially grown—and never dig up plants from the wild yourself.

ASTER
Aster species

Asters flourish in sunny plots of regularly irrigated, fertile soil. Breeders have seized on their natural suitability as garden plants and developed a large range of cultivars, commonly known as Michaelmas daisies. Asters are loved for their late flowers. Myriad pink, blue, violet, purple or white daisies open at the very end of summer. Most of the species are *herbaceous perennials;* the stems die back in winter and regrow each spring. Taller asters may need support to stop the stems from tumbling over. To reduce the risk of mildew, water asters at the base, keeping the leaves and stems dry. Divide asters (see page 39) every few years for an abundance of new plants.

Native New England aster, *A. novae-angliae,* is one of the parents of the Michaelmas daisy cultivars, with particularly large, showy flowers that bloom as early as August. It originates in moist areas from the eastern states to New Mexico and in the garden does best in damp soil.

GARDEN DESIGN

Just because a goal of a wildflower gardener is to mimic nature, it doesn't mean that the garden can be planted without some planning. Designing a garden is an art based on the same principles as other types of art. These principles are form, scale, rhythm, axis, color and texture. *Form* is the shape and structure of the elements. Too much of one form will be monotonous; too many different forms can become confusing. Vertical forms present a sense of awe; horizontal forms, peacefulness; straight lines, reason; intricate forms, curiosity; curves, harmony; circular forms, closure; jagged forms, power.

Scale refers to relative size. When choosing the size of patios, paths and planting beds and borders, consider the size of the house and lot and the needs of the people using it.

Rhythm refers to ordering elements in the garden, like beats in music. Give your yard rhythm by repeating the same wildflowers in several areas of the garden or using the same construction materials in several areas.

Axis gives the garden visual orientation, forcing people to look at what you want them to see. Axis is formed by paths, paving patterns, lighting and plants that hide, frame or create views.

There are many ways to use *color* in the garden: Plant wildflowers to coordinate with the trim color of the house; use the same color palette outdoors as in the house interior to unify the two areas; plant many different wildflowers of similar bloom color for brilliant splashes of color or plant drifts of flowers with contrasting blooms to make each stand out. Be sure to consider how both the blooms and leaves of different wildflowers will work together.

Texture refers to the tactile surfaces of all materials used in your design. Combine different textures to add interest. Small spaces are more conducive to fine-textured elements, larger ones to coarser textures.

BEE BALM
Monarda didyma

SCARLET WHORLS

Bee balm was one of the many exotic wild-flowers early explorers took from the New World back to Europe and it is still the mainstay of many English perennial flower borders. Kept moist, bee balm is magnificent as a border plant. In dry conditions it becomes scraggly, but can be the backbone of a woodland garden (see page 49) when left to run wild with other moisture-loving plants in a damp or constantly wet piece of ground.

Water and at least four hours of sunlight a day are the keys to growing bee balm successfully. A native of the eastern woodlands, it will tolerate partial shade. In areas not naturally moist, weekly or even twice-weekly waterings are necessary through the summer.

A member of the mint family, bee balm has square stalks and spreads rapidly by branching underground stems, called *runners* or *rhizomes*. In fertile soil, the plants will grow luxuriantly and the runners will run wild. Either lift and divide the plants every spring (see page 39) before the new growth appears, discarding all but a few pieces of each plant, or grow bee balm in a container sunk into the ground, so the runners stay contained.

Bee balm's magnificent red-hued flowers, which open in pompons, or whorls, for three to five weeks in July on towering four- or even six-foot stalks, attract hummingbirds, bees and butterflies. The blooms make long-lasting cut flowers.

Japanese beetles eat bee balm leaves, and mildew grows on the leaves. If unsightly, cut back the plants to six inches and wait a few weeks for new shoots to appear.

The other common name for bee balm is Oswego tea. The Oswego Indians reputedly steeped the leaves to make tea and soothe bee stings.

BELLFLOWER, HAREBELL
Campanula rotundifolia

SUMMER BELLS

Bellflower's slender stems and delicate flowers belie its extreme hardiness and adaptability. Every spring, it breaks through the soil on windy, snow-strewn slopes in Scotland and Alaska, as well as in its native Rockies. Although summers are cool in most of its native range, bellflower, also known as harebell, will tolerate heat if you keep it watered.

There are many garden uses for bellflower. It is sufficiently stunning for a place in a sunny rock garden or a patio container. Alternatively, show off its graceful tumbling habit by planting groups at the front of a border or along a walkway. Massing it on a sunny slope is also effective. The first nodding flowers open in June, and the plants keep flowering until September. Flower color varies from violet to lavender to white.

Bellflower suits all garden soils except extremely dry or constantly wet soils. If the soil is not well drained, mix in a shovelful of organic material at planting time. Choose a sunny space for this plant, and keep it tidy and blooming prolifically by fertilizing it through the summer. Bellflower appreciates regular watering but will tolerate dry periods once it is established. Strong winds usually stunt garden plants or blow them down; bellflower is an exception, easily withstanding exposed, windy conditions.

Divide bellflower every few years to maintain its vigor. Lift the plants in spring and separate them into large pieces (see page 39), then replant the pieces a foot apart with the foliage at the soil surface and the swollen roots, or rhizomes, an inch below the surface.

Bellflower, also known as harebell, grows to about 12 in. Its dainty, showy habit and cultural adaptability make it suitable for a wide range of garden uses.

CREATING A WILD DESIGN

There are many ways to use wildflowers beautifully. Most important is that your garden design fit your house style. Wildflowers are the obvious choice for flower-filled cottage gardens surrounding a rustic-style home. Equally effective is a formal pattern of a few wildflowers, arranged symmetrically, in front of a Victorian-style home or a low, horizontal line of mounding wildflowers along the foundations of a ranch-style home. A "wild" garden need not be an unruly helter-skelter arrangement that irritates the neighbors, but can be a beautiful, natural showpiece.

For best results, design the area for your wildflowers using the basic principles of design: form, scale, rhythm, axis, color and texture (see page 7). These principles govern the overall shape of the garden area and its relation to the rest of the yard.

Always review when each plant will flower, its full growth height, the flower color, the leaf color and texture and how it will look with established plants. This will help you create a garden that is coordinated to your house and yard and provides you with a festival of color for the entire blooming season.

Wildflowers are especially effective in low beds or borders next to lawns or fronting evergreen trees and shrubs. Look for tall plants for the back of a border bed or center of an island bed and low-growing ones for the front. Unless it is a bold accent plant, think twice before placing a single plant by itself; clusters of three or five make a more natural and effective arrangement. For an informal look, avoid straight lines, and if there's space, repeat groups of plants to mimic the drifts of flowers in nature.

For great effect, look for and copy plant combinations that occur in nature:
• Bluebells and ferns
• Coneflower, gay-feather and grasses
• Lupines and California poppies

BLACK-EYED SUSAN
Rudbeckia fulgida

PRAIRIE RUNAWAY

Black-eyed Susan is a familiar sight along thousands of miles of roadside in summer. Originally it was simply a prairie flower, but apparently seeds were mistakenly shipped with clover to farmers in the East, and black-eyed Susan became established in eastern farmlands. Now it has naturalized in most states, including Hawaii, where it grows so well that it is considered a nuisance.

Although its persistent reseeding and adaptability to a range of conditions has earned this plant the status of weed in some places, it's a beautiful wildflower for the garden. Its stiff, bristly one- to three-foot stems and brilliant golden flowers with dark brown-purple centers are sufficiently remarkable to serve as a garden focus. Place a single plant at the center of a small border or in a container close to the house. Or plant a mass of black-eyed Susan for a stunning sweep of color.

While the *R. fulgida* is a perennial, the very similar looking *R. hirta,* also called black-eyed Susan, is an annual. Whether plants survive from year to year depends on winter conditions. However, it is easy to keep a supply of black-eyed Susan going in your garden: the plants self-sow abundantly, so carpets of seedlings will most likely sprout every spring and be in flower by summer.

As long as it gets plenty of sunshine, this is a truly adaptable plant. Heavy or light soil, rich or infertile soil, regular watering or very little watering: any combination suits perky black-eyed Susan.

Black-eyed Susan flowers from June through July and then, if picked, intermittently until a heavy frost. The festive blooms last well as cut flowers.

13

BLANKET FLOWER
Gaillardia species

STURDY CUT FLOWER

Heat and drought and poor soil are harsh conditions for most flowers, but blanket flower thrives in them. Sown or planted in spring, these stocky, sprawling plants with one- to two-foot stems will produce dozens of yellow-and-red blooms from the beginning of summer until the first frost.

Blanket flower is one of the easiest wild-flowers to raise from seed (see page 27). Sow the seed any time in spring or even early summer; they will germinate quickly. Alternatively, start from young plants. Many nurseries carry one of the blanket flower natives alongside the even brighter cultivars developed by plant breeders.

The most common natives are *G. aristata,* a perennial shown in the photograph, and *G. pulchella,* an annual. Both plants are best started from new plants or seeds each year, because they do not self-sow reliably and the perennial is only reliably perennial along the California and Gulf coasts.

Blanket flower has two cultural require-ments: sun and well-drained soil. In a sunny garden with heavy soil, add peat, leaf mold or compost to the planting hole to improve drainage. For shady gardens, choose a differ-ent plant to avoid disappointment.

Snipping off the flower heads as they fade, called *deadheading,* ensures a continuous supply of summer flowers. Plant blanket flower in groups and keep picking the cheery blooms for indoor flower arrangements. Blanket flower grows wild in most regions of the United States. It is an excellent plant for coastal (see page 23), prairie (see page 41) and

The name *blanket flower* derives from the jagged pattern on the petal edges, reminiscent of Native American blanket designs.

PREPARING THE SOIL

The wildflowers featured in this book are easy to grow in standard garden soils. If you already have flowers or vegetables growing well in your garden, you will have no trouble with wildflowers. If you are planning a wildflower garden on neglected ground, first you will need to deal with weeds and decide whether to improve the soil.

To keep unwanted weeds from overrunning a wildflower garden, clear them and any dormant weed seed from your site. First, turn over the soil to a depth of eight inches, then water thoroughly and wait a few weeks for the weed seeds to germinate. Once they do, clear them, water the soil, and wait a few weeks for the second crop of weeds. Clear that second crop also before sowing wildflower seeds or setting out wildflower plants. If you are planting a large site and the tilling and retilling are too time consuming, you can clear the weeds once and scratch seed into the surface without tilling, but the results may not be as rewarding. Herbicides will save you work clearing weeds, but they do not kill weed seeds. Choose a nonresidual herbicide, and follow the directions carefully.

Many garden soils will need no further preparation, especially if you select wildflowers suited to your soil (see page 19). To improve clay soils, extremely sandy soils and infertile soils, dig in *organic material* such as compost, leaf mold or manure. Organic material aerates heavy soils, improving the drainage, and binds light soils, improving their moisture-retaining ability. It also contains nutrients, which are released in decomposition.

Before committing to a major soil improvement project, read the plant descriptions in this book. You will find beautiful wildflowers that naturally thrive in infertile, sandy and even soggy soils.

BLEEDING HEART
Dicentra species

Bleeding heart's ferny leaves and delicate, arching sprays of heart-shaped flowers soften a woodland garden and make a striking rock garden or container plant. Plant bleeding hearts in rich soil with lots of organic material and water regularly so the soil never dries out completely. Shade is essential; in direct sun the leaves turn an anemic yellow-green and the flowers come to nothing. Bleeding hearts are perennials. Some lose their foliage in summer, but new leaves sprout the following spring. In cold-winter areas, cover with a couple of inches of mulch in fall to help them survive severe freezes.

Fringed bleeding heart, *D. eximia*, blooms the longest of any bleeding heart, from early spring until fall. It grows to 2 ft. and retains its pretty foliage through the summer. This eastern woodland native prefers a slightly acid soil.

Dutchman's breeches
D. cucullaria
So-named because of its pantaloon-shaped flowers, Dutchman's breeches makes an airy, 6 to 10 inch high carpet in partial or deep shade. The flowers bloom for just 2 weeks in April or May. A few weeks later, the foliage dies back and will regrow the following spring only if the roots get several months of minimum temperatures below 40°F. It is native to the eastern and northwestern states.

Western bleeding heart
D. formosa
Western bleeding heart grows to 18 in. and flowers from March until July. The flowers may be purple, rose or white; the leaves are blue-green. Native to moist West Coast woodlands, Western bleeding heart tolerates heat better than other bleeding hearts. Unlike most bleeding hearts, it quickly spreads.

BUNCHBERRY
Cornus canadensis

Bunchberry's cream "flowers" (actually leaf bracts—the tiny, greenish white flowers are in the center) last from June through August. As they fade, vivid orange-red berries form among the leaves, which turn yellow and red in fall. Native to cool, damp woodlands, bunchberry is not a good choice for a sunny garden; the deeper the shade, the deeper green the leaves. Its cold-winter requirement makes it a common sight in Minnesota and Alaska. It must have constantly moist, well-drained, slightly acidic soil. To increase the acidity of your soil, add sphagnum moss to the soil and apply two inches of pine needles on the soil surface. Bunchberry spreads quickly by underground runners, which you can lift in spring or fall, cut and replant to form new colonies.

Only 6 in., bunchberry is a choice ground cover for moist, shady gardens. Its many charming characteristics include lovely flowers, brilliant fruits and handsome green leaves that change color in fall.

CHOOSING PLANTS

It is tempting to pick up the prettiest plants or seed packets at the nursery and then look for a spot to put them in. But beautiful gardens are built with some forethought. Take 15 minutes to consider the best wildflowers for your garden before you start shopping.

The most successful gardens are planned with the *cultural requirements*—sun, soil and water needs—of the plants in mind. As you read the plant descriptions, look for the set of clues that indicate how easily each plant will grow in your site. As a rule of thumb, there are two broad categories of wildflowers: those that thrive in sunny sites with poor soil and little irrigation, often the prairie wildflowers such as blanket flower, and those that love shady sites with rich soil and plenty of moisture, often the woodland plants such as bunchberry. Determine quickly, without pursuing a detailed analysis, which plant type best suits your climate and the spot you are about to plant, and then choose among plants of that type.

Matching plants to your site conditions will save soil preparation, maintenance time and frustration. In an exposed hot, dry garden, woodland plants are likely to fail however frequently you drag around the hoses. Yet on the cool, shady north side of a building in that same garden, you could grow woodland plants quite successfully provided you enriched the soil and kept it moist.

Study which flowers are growing well in local wild areas. You cannot go wrong by selecting plants native to your area and mimicking their growing environment. At the nursery, reject plants that are pale, *pot-bound* (have roots growing through the drainage holes) or show signs of pests or disease. Buy wildflower seed or plants from nurseries and catalogs that clearly state they raise their own wildflowers. Never dig up plants from the wild.

BUTTERFLY WEED
Asclepias tuberosa

SUMMER COLOR

Half its name is appropriate. Butterfly weed attracts swarms of butterflies all summer. It is a major food source for the monarch butterfly, and occasionally butterfly larvae will strip this wildflower to its bare stems. But it is not a weed. It grows tidily, one to three feet, and keeps within proper bounds.

Its long-lasting, vibrant, dazzling flowers make butterfly weed popular among gardeners all over the United States. Surrounded by rich green grass or planted against a dark hedge, it draws attention even at a distance. Among equally vivid wildflowers, such as bee balm and black-eyed Susan, its flat-topped flower clusters make a pretty contrast.

Bright orange butterfly weed is native to the western deserts, the Great Plains and the southern and eastern states. It is an excellent choice for a prairie garden (see page 41). Grow in any sunny place with well-drained, average soil. Like several other wildflowers in this book, once it is established it thrives on benign neglect. It is drought tolerant, and there is no need to fertilize it because it prefers infertile soil. In rich or damp soil, its thick tuberous root will rot.

Cut the first flush of flowers in June to encourage the plant to keep blooming. The flowers will last a week in an indoor arrangement. If aphids or mildew make the plants unsightly at any time during the summer, trim them back to six inches; they will produce new flower buds within a few weeks. Butterfly weed dries beautifully, retaining much of its flamboyant color. The occasional five-inch, beige seed pod is also worth preserving for dried arrangements (see page 61).

Although a member of the milkweed family, bright orange butterfly weed does not have the characteristic white, milky sap. In fall it does produce stunning, long milkweed pods full of silky down seeds.

21

CALIFORNIA POPPY
Eschscholzia californica

On the West Coast, California poppy carpets the hillsides from February through spring and far into summer. It will open a little later in gardens in cold-winter regions, but you can count on it blooming until September if watered occasionally. California poppy is prolific and adaptable. Sow seeds in spring, or fall on the West Coast, directly where you want the plants to grow (see page 27). They do not transplant well because, like carrots and butterfly weed, they have a single long *taproot*—a long slender root that grows deeply downward—that is easily broken. Choose a sunny location where the soil is only moderately fertile, not rich. Water the plants until they are well established, then only as necessary to prolong blooming. California poppies are low-growing (under two feet) tender perennials; they overwinter only in very mild climates. In cold regions, start them from seed each year.

California poppy's satiny petals are bright orange to yellow. Plant it in broad sweeps on a sunny slope or in a border or a coastal garden. Its vivid color covers hillsides all spring and summer, giving rise to California's nickname, the Golden State.

A Coastal Garden

Creating a wildflower garden at the coast is easier than it might at first appear. There are numerous plants that can tolerate strong winds, salt spray, fog and sandy or rocky soil. The many vibrant ones, including California poppy and blanket flower, make a dazzling pattern against an expanse of blue ocean.

Before setting out wildflowers in a coastal site, consider placing a few tall shrubs on the windward side of the garden to protect the flowers from wind. Plant native grasses to anchor the soil and blend the garden into the landscape. Sea oats, *Chasmanthium latifolium,* is commonly used for this purpose in Gulf Coast gardens; American beach grass, *Ammophila breviligulata,* in gardens next to the Atlantic and European beach grass, *A. arenaria,* in West Coast gardens.

For best results, start by mixing organic matter into the soil before planting. Seaweed—first rinsed to remove the salt—makes excellent compost mixed with garden clippings free of weeds and kitchen waste free of rodent-attracting animal fat. Water new plantings frequently until they are established; sand is extremely fast- draining, and wind can desiccate a plant before it develops an extensive root system. Fertilize coastal gardens occasionally to compensate for the nutrient-poor soil.

Plants that thrive in the harsh conditions of coastal gardens are often, of necessity, low-growing and sturdy, but they are no less beautiful for that. You can construct a delicate, richly perfumed garden on a windy seaside site—or hundreds of miles from the ocean around a clapboard cottage on a naturally sandy or rocky soil—with white evening primrose and its relative clarkia planted among soft native grasses, driftwood and sand. If a kaleidoscope of bright color is more in keeping with your home style and desires, plant California poppies, lupines, penstemons and asters.

COASTAL WILDFLOWERS

Aster
Blanket flower
California poppy
Clarkia
Lupine
Penstemon
White and desert evening
   primroses

CARDINAL FLOWER
Lobelia species

HUMMINGBIRD JEWEL

Hummingbirds home in on red flowers.
Because of this, they visit red wild columbine
in early summer, then look for the red whorls
of bee balm or the brilliant scarlet spikes of
cardinal flower. As they lick the nectar out of
the tubular flowers with their long tongues,
their heads dust pollen off the anthers onto
the stigmas, pollinating the flowers.

Great blue lobelia, *L. siphilitica*, below, a
relative of cardinal flower, tolerates dryness
a little better than cardinal flower, but
neither flower is a wise choice for dry areas.
Plant these wildflowers in a naturally moist
area or in a border that you keep constantly
damp, such as a wetland garden. Partial
shade suits them best, but they do tolerate
full sun and heat if kept fairly moist.
Plant them in soil rich in organic material,
and divide the fast-growing clumps every
two years.

Both cardinal flower and great blue lobelia
are eye-catchers. They grow to three or four
feet, and a group of just three will make a
bold display in midsummer and early fall.
They are native to the eastern states.

WETLAND WILDFLOWERS

Bee balm
Cardinal flower
Lilies
Moisture-loving iris

A Wetland Garden

Soggy ground is problematic for most plants. The vast majority of wildflowers need well-drained soil to grow. Their roots require oxygen, which is unavailable in constantly wet soils, so they drown. If you have a patch of land that never dries out, rather than fighting nature with shovelfuls of soil amendments, consider emphasizing its wetness and seeking out the many unusual, often dramatically textured plants that will thrive there.

Cardinal flower, great blue lobelia, bee balm, and many native irises and lilies appreciate wet soil. A large planting of one of these wildflowers along a wet ditch or swale will immediately turn it into the garden's focal point. For a bold, textural planting, consider adding any of the other plants in the list on page 24.

Most moisture-loving plants prefer rich, woodsy soil. If your soil is not spongy with organic materials, add peat moss or sphagnum moss. Check your wetland garden regularly during the summer, and top it off with water if the soil starts to dry out.

A small wetland garden can be created anywhere by lining an 18-inch-deep hole with a PVC tarp punctured with an occasional drainage hole and filling it with saturated soil rich in organic material. This is an interesting project for gardens that are moist much of the year. In arid regions a drip irrigation system could keep the soil wet, but water is usually too precious to use in this way, and woodland plants tend to look unnatural in arid surroundings.

One or two containers of wetland plants make a fascinating display for a deck or patio garden. Fill the containers with a mix of sand and peat moss, and choose deep saucers or containers with just a single drainage hole to retain as much moisture in the soil as you can. Water frequently, of course.

Cardinal flower, *L. cardinalis,* loves moisture around its roots but not overhead watering, which may cause leaf and stem spot.

25

CLARKIA
Clarkia species

Named after the explorer William Clark, who crossed the Rocky Mountains in 1806, clarkias are native to California, but have naturalized throughout the West and will grow in all the continental states. Seek out the satiny-flowered native clarkia or purchase the double-flowered hybrids, *C. unquiculata*, common in garden centers. It blooms in shades of red, pink, lavender and white from June to August. Choose a sunny site. In very hot climates, water the plants regularly through the summer.

Clarkias are annuals and easy to grow from seed. They are drought tolerant once they start to flower—within 3 months of sowing—and grow readily in thin, unfertilized, light soils, making them ideal for both coastal and desert gardens (see pages 23 and 57).

Starting From Seed

First For the best germination results, start with fresh seed from a reputable supplier and check the seed packet for the use date. Many annuals bloom within 3 months.

Fourth Cover the area with a light layer of soil, about ⅛ in. deep, to keep the seed from drying out. A thicker covering may prevent the seeds from germinating.

Then Add organic material only if the seed packet recommends rich soil. Break up the top 6 in. of soil with a trowel or spade, remove any weeds and rake the soil until smooth.

Next Tamp the area firmly with the rake, tines flat against the soil. Germination times vary greatly according to the wildflower and the soil conditions.

Third Sow the seed in drifts for a natural, wild effect. Place large seeds in position; mix small seeds with damp fine sand so that you can scatter them more evenly.

Last Water with a fine spray immediately after sowing, and keep the soil moist until the plants are established. Even drought-tolerant natives need water to get started.

COLUMBINE
Aquilegia species

SLENDER SPURS OF NECTAR

From April through June, columbines are at their peak. Bumblebees and butterflies work through the flowers constantly, seeking the nectar in the long spurs that sweep straight back from the petals. If you watch for a while, you will see some insects taking short-cuts, nibbling off the spur ends rather than crawling through the flowers.

Columbine is one of America's most instantly recognizable wildflowers. There is a native columbine growing wild in almost every region of the continent, and these are often available at nurseries alongside the new, double-flowered hybrid columbines. The native columbines are just as beautiful as the modern cultivars.

Gardeners usually associate columbine with woodland plantings. A mass of columbine certainly is showy against a shady, deep green background of ferns and shrubs, but consider them too for a rock garden, where they will quickly reseed themselves into crevices. They also make elegant pondside plants.

Columbines adapt to a variety of soils and light conditions. Avoid planting them in poorly drained soil or in very rich soils, where the foliage will flourish but the blooms will be few. In hot-summer regions, place in a partially shady area and keep the plants watered. In any region, weekly watering will produce lush plants with flowers for long-lasting indoor arrangements.

Columbines are perennials. The foliage dies back in cold-winter areas but will reemerge in spring. They also self-sow, spreading through the garden to form a very attractive colony within a few years.

Wild columbine, *A. canadensis*, grows in meadows and open woodlands in the eastern half of the United States. Its delicate, nodding flower stems may reach 3 ft. in the garden.

28

Blue columbine
A. caerulea

From a distance, this Colorado native looks uniformly pale blue. On closer analysis the white, violet and yellow details become clear and all the flowers are different shades. The stems grow to 2½ ft. The flowers open in June and continue through August.

Golden columbine
A. chrysantha

Plant golden columbine in a woodland setting or in clusters in a flower border, where its 4-ft. flowering stems will make quite an impact. A native of the Southwest, golden columbine tolerates dry soil more easily than the other columbines. It flowers from April to August and is fragrant.

CONEFLOWER
Ratibida species

SUMMER CUT FLOWERS

Reflexed petals and a pronounced cone, often with a ribbon of dark red, give coneflower its other common name: Mexican hat. Most members of the daisy family have two types of flowers, ray flowers and disk flowers; coneflower shares the familial yellow ray flowers, but instead of the typical yellow disk flowers has clusters of tiny, rusty brown flowers on a magnificent cone.

Native originally to the Great Plains, western deserts and Midwest, but now growing wild in most parts of the country, coneflower blooms all summer long in dry, sun-drenched soil, making it a good choice for a desert garden (see page 57). It is a hardy wildflower that is easy to grow in a garden and thrives on little attention. Fuss over it with a watering can or plant it in rich soil, and it will probably rot. In very cold winter regions, where temperatures fall below −20° F, protect plants for the winter with a four-inch cover of leaves or compost.

Coneflower is a natural choice for a mixed border. It provides constant bold color for months, then as the last flowers fade and the plant turns nondescript, the more attractive surrounding perennials and shrubs will assume the focus of attention.

The seeds germinate in five to ten days, but then you need a little patience, because the plants will wait until their second year to flower. A patch of coneflower and Queen Anne's lace makes a simple but lovely prairie garden—and provides an abundance of cut flowers through the summer.

Coneflower, *R. columnifera*, grows best in dry, poor soils, where it reaches 3 ft. Its bold flowers attract both bees and butterflies.

Prairie coneflower
R. pinnata
An especially striking species with purple cones and stems that shoot up to 5 ft. It tolerates alkaline and clay soils. Give prairie coneflower plenty of growing room.

CORALBELLS
Heuchera species

EVERGREEN ROSETTES

Coralbells are handsome the year around, never losing their leaves untidily after flowering as many traditional border plants do. In fall, when companion plants such as lilies are best cut back and camouflaged, coralbells continue as neat rosettes of heart-shaped leaves, often with fabulous mottling in shades of white, silver and maroon. If temperatures fall below 10° F, coralbells will die back.

Plant coralbells in groups in flower beds so that the dainty, wandlike flower stems together produce an airy effect. Or plant them singly in a rock garden or container, where their beautiful leaf and flower details will be noticed. Coralbells are commonly planted as an edging around rose beds. It is native to the Southwest. Hummingbirds are drawn to the pink-and-red flowers. Bees pollinate them. The long, leafless stems flower for weeks through the summer, especially if you pick the faded flowers.

Coralbells are native to moist, shady areas making them good subjects for a shady flower border or a woodland garden that receives regular watering in the summer. They will tolerate a range of conditions, including full sun, dry soil and even heat if they receive regular watering. Poor soil is sufficient for most species; however, it must be well drained to avoid problems with crown rot, a fungus that kills the heart of the plant.

Like many other clump-forming plants, coralbells can be divided. Three years after planting, in spring or fall, dig up the plants, tease apart pieces and replant them with the buds at the soil surface (see page 39).

Heuchera sanguinea, the plant most commonly called coralbells, produces loose clusters of salmon to bright red flowers from April to August. The leaves form neat 6-in.-high rosettes; the flower stems reach 2 ft.

Alumroot
H. americana

A cousin of coralbells, alumroot or rock geranium flowers in late spring; its flowers are usually pink or purple. Attractive white, silver, bronze or maroon spots may mottle the mature leaves, especially if the plant receives some direct sun. The leaves form a 1½-ft.-tall mound, the flower stems reach 3 ft. Alumroot is native to the eastern states.

Small-flowered alumroot
H. micrantha

Another coralbells relative, small-flowered alumroot grows to 2 ft. Its tiny flowers appear in great numbers and are usually white, pale pink or a fascinating pale green. It is native to the West Coast mountains.

COREOPSIS
Coreopsis species

SUNNY DISKS

One of the best uses for coreopsis is as a trail-blazer. It will turn a new wildflower garden into a swath of sunny flowers in the very first summer. It grows quickly from seed. Sow it in spring (leaving the seed uncovered, see page 27), and it will germinate in one week and produce flowers within three months. By fall, the seed will be ripening for an even larger colony the following year.

Coreopsis produces a profusion of flowers all summer. If you remove each flush of blooms as they fade, many types of coreopsis will keep flowering from May through August. The flowers top long, slender stems and last a long time as cut flowers.

All types of coreopsis are easy to grow in sunny gardens. They thrive in any well-drained soil, including thin, dry soils, and all tolerate heat. Keep the ground moist during germination and the seedling stage, then cut back the irrigation schedule to as little as an occasional watering in the driest periods.

There are a hundred different kinds of coreopsis, with wide native ranges. Many are southern or eastern natives, but all grow anywhere in the United States. Lance-leaved coreopsis, *C. lanceolata,* is the most common prairie coreopsis. It is a perennial, forming fast-growing, two-foot-tall clumps, which can be divided in spring for new plantings. It also self-sows as rampantly as the annual types. The sea dahlia, *C. maritima,* is an early-spring-flowering California perennial that reseeds successfully from year to year in colder regions. For a partially shaded garden, seek out eared coreopsis, *C. auriculata.*

Plains coreopsis
C. tinctoria
A distinctive annual, plains coreopsis has soft, ferny foliage and striking bicolor petals around a maroon disk. Plants grow to 3 ft., but are narrow, so space them closely for a solid mass. Wild in many regions of the country, it is less drought tolerant than other forms of coreopsis.

Lance-leaved coreopsis, *C. lanceolata,* like all the other coreopsis, spreads rapidly. Mass it along a sunny walkway. It blooms for months, and its seedheads attract birds.

EVENING PRIMROSE
Oenothera species

Evening primroses are charming wildflowers. The loose, billowy plants produce silky flowers, often fragrant, over many months, and the plants are drought tolerant, easy to grow in sunny gardens and especially useful in hot, dry areas, such as desert gardens (see page 57). They also attract birds and bees. The flowers of evening primrose open at dusk and close again at dawn. There are day-flowering types called sundrops. All are simple to grow from seed, but some do not flower until the second year. Some evening primroses become rampant in rich garden soil.

Hooker's evening primrose
O. hookeri
Hooker's evening primrose has red stems and grows from 1 to 6 ft. It will tolerate dry soil but grows better in moist ground. Because it is a biennial, sow seeds or set out young nursery plants in two consecutive years. That way, you will have flowers all summer every year. This evening primrose is native to many western states.

Desert evening primrose
O. deltoides
Desert evening primrose, a native of the western deserts, is the most drought-tolerant evening primrose. Plant it in sand or on any arid ground that is well-drained, and it will thrive. Use it as a ground cover in a coastal garden (see page 23) for spring color. It grows just a few inches tall, is a perennial and flowers from March to June, making it one of the earliest-flowering evening primroses.

Missouri evening primrose
O. missouriensis
A small perennial, 8 to 10 in., Missouri evening primrose is an ideal ground cover or rock garden plant for sunny gardens. From May until October, it produces very large yellow flowers that fade to red. This midwestern native needs very well drained soil.

Ozark sundrops
O. fruticosa
Ozark sundrops grow well in partial shade as well as in very sunny places. The flowers, which open during the day, last for just a few weeks starting in midspring; the leaves are spotted maroon. Ozark sundrops grow to 2 or 3 ft. It is a perennial and a native of the eastern states. To prevent the crown from rotting, avoid overwatering.

Tufted evening primrose
O. caespitosa
Tufted evening primrose makes a charming perennial ground cover or container plant. Its large fragrant flowers age from white to pink and then red. Each flower lasts only one night, but the plants are covered in flowers from May until fall. Keep this western native relatively dry.

Showy evening primrose
O. speciosa
Showy evening primrose, a native of the prairies, has blue-green leaves and slightly scented flowers that fade from pink to white. Unlike the other evening primroses, it flowers by day. It is a fairly low growing perennial, about 1½ ft. Plants bloom in midsummer for a month or more.

White evening primrose
O. pallida
Another fragrant native from the western states, white evening primrose reaches a little over a foot high. It is an attractive perennial for the front or middle of a border or massed on a bank. It tolerates salt spray, making it reliable for coastal gardens. The flowers are sometimes streaked lightly with lavender.

FALSE MITERWORT
Tiarella cordifolia

One of the easiest and prettiest ground covers for a woodland or rock garden, false miterwort produces new bright green foliage each spring and foamy spires of white flowers by early spring. The foliage turns red and withers in fall or early spring, depending on winter cold. Plant false miterwort in partial shade and moist soil that is rich in organic material. It grows wild in the damp woodlands and stream banks of Nova Scotia, Michigan and Alabama. Other members of the *tiarella* species are known commonly as foam flowers.

False miterwort spreads by runners, like strawberries, making a dense carpet in any shady, moist garden within two or three years.

Dividing Herbaceous Plants

First Dig up the entire clump with its rootball. Many clumping perennials, such as false miterwort, aster, cardinal flower, coneflower and coralbells (shown here) divide easily and make interesting gifts for friends and neighbors. Divide spring-flowering clumps in fall and fall-flowering clumps in early spring before growth starts.

Third Cut back any broken or bruised leaves, stems and roots. On a warm or windy day, either wait until evening before you start dividing plants or be sure to cover the divisions with damp newspaper after you lift them from the ground and keep them covered until you are ready to plant them. The roots must not dry out.

Then Shake the clump free of soil. If the soil is wet and muddy, gently hose it away from the roots. Tease apart large pieces from the center of the plant. Cut away the pieces with a knife if necessary. Dividing a clump into a few large pieces will give strong new plants; small pieces will take longer to establish.

Last Dig new holes and replant the divisions immediately, placing them at the same depth as the original plant. Firm the soil around each plant, and water regularly until the plants are established. Many perennials grow more vigorously and flower more prolifically if divided every 3 years.

GAY-FEATHERS
Liatris species

PRAIRIE SPIKES

Few plants are easier to grow than gay-feathers. They need full sun to keep their stems strong and straight and reasonably well drained soil to prevent root rot in winter. If you choose the tallest native gay-feathers, which reach four feet, you may need to stake the stems (see page 55) so they do not tumble. Otherwise gay-feathers are undemanding. They thrive in ordinary or even poor garden soil and tolerate heat and drought. Spoiling them with enriched soil or regular watering may produce limp, untidy plants (*L. pycnostachya* needs a little more moisture than the others).

The first flowers to open are the ones at the very tip of the spike, then the flowers below unfold, which is an unusual order for spike flowers. The plants bloom for many weeks in midsummer; some kinds flower into fall. Mature clumps may produce more than a dozen flower spikes a few years after planting. Butterflies love the velvety flowers.

Scatter gay-feathers among goldenrod, coneflower and black-eyed Susan, where their rigid purple or lavender spikes will provide a striking contrast to the billowy masses of yellow flowers. They are equally dramatic grouped toward the rear of a border.

Gay-feathers make long-lasting cut flowers, and they dry well too if you cut them as they start to flower (see page 61). Once the plants have finished flowering, cut off the faded stems; the grassy foliage is inconspicuous. Gay-feathers are native to many states in the East, South and Midwest.

Blazing star, *L. spicata,* is one of the tallest gay-feathers. It reaches 4 ft. in ordinary soil with occasional watering. In dry sites it makes a more compact but still very attractive plant that is a perfect accent for a prairie garden.

A PRAIRIE GARDEN

A prairie garden is most wildflower gardeners' dream: a meadow of delicate grasses and flowers—reminiscent of the millions of lost acres of pristine American prairie—dancing in a warm breeze. Prairie gardens are exceptionally beautiful, but they demand regular attention for the first few years. The challenge is to replicate the colorful diversity of annuals and perennials found in the prairies.

Commercial wildflower meadow seed mixes can be an easy way to start a prairie garden. Before sowing a mix, check that it contains the diversity you want for your design and that all of the plants suit the growing conditions of your site.

For a prairie garden, choose a site that receives full sun all day. In early spring or fall, sow or plant an even spread of small, noninvasive native grasses, such as little bluestem, *Schizachyrium scoparium,* which turns a pretty bronze in fall. Grasses are the foundation of a prairie garden; they provide its characteristic airiness and grace.

In between the grasses, sow drifts of one or two medium-height annuals that will reseed themselves, for example, coreopsis or lupine. These annuals will give a quick spread of color while the perennials get established. The fastest way to establish perennials is to purchase plants; most take two years to flower from seed. Buy plants of just two or three types of perennials, unless your garden is quite large, and plug them into the seeded area either in clusters or scattered.

Keep the soil moist until the seeds germinate, and water regularly throughout the first year. Keep watch over the plant mix, removing weeds as they appear and wildflower seedlings that are becoming too dominant.

The incidental rewards of a beautiful prairie garden include butterflies, armfuls of cut flowers throughout the summer, and a place to work in and study the cycles of flowers, seeds, rest and renewal.

PRAIRIE WILDFLOWERS

Aster
Bee balm
Bird's foot violet
Blanket flower
Butterfly weed
Coneflower
Evening primrose
Gay-feather
Goldenrod
Lupine
Pasque flower
Sunflower

GERANIUM
Geranium species

Geraniums are excellent wildflowers to integrate into an existing irrigated garden. They form airy, one- to two-foot-tall masses of pretty flowers and handsome foliage, and they will grow profusely in any average garden soil that receives regular watering. Place them singly in a sunny rock garden (see page 63) or in groups of three or more at the front of a partially shaded woodland garden (see page 49). In spring and fall, mulch them with decomposing leaves. Bleeding heart, phlox, ferns and cardinal flower work well planted with native geraniums.

Wild geranium, *G. maculatum,* grows in open woods and damp meadows in the East and Midwest. It propagates by seed and rhizomes, flowering from April to May.

Planting Transplants

First Because many wildflowers are being illegally dug from the wild, ask about the source and buy only commercially grown plants. Never dig plants from their native habitat.

Then Keep potted transplants watered. Transplant early or late in the day, when plants will suffer less shock. Choose a site that suits the plants' cultural requirements.

Third If necessary amend the soil. Using a trowel, dig a hole wider than and about as deep as the pot. Space the plants so that each has plenty of room to grow.

Fourth Loosely holding the plant, gently slide it out of its pot. Retain as much of the soil around the roots as you can. If the plant sticks in the pot, lightly tap the sides and bottom.

Next Place the plant in the hole, and fill in around it with soil. Check that the plant is at the same depth as it was in its pot. Press the soil firmly around the plant.

Last Water thoroughly, being careful not to splash the leaves. Keep the plants well watered; even drought-tolerant plants need regular watering until they are established.

GOLDENROD
Solidago species

BACK OF THE BORDER

Goldenrod has an ill-deserved reputation as a common weed and the source of fall hay fever. Actually, the hay fever culprit is the somewhat similar-looking giant ragweed. In Europe, gardeners treasure North American goldenrods. They plant these tall plants at the rear of flower borders, glad of their exceptional showiness in fall when most other border flowers have faded.

There are about 90 native goldenrods. Some are loose, shrubby plants towering to nine feet; some are low-growing ground covers. The few fragrant ones smell of anise. Foliage ranges from green to bronze and gray. All are remarkably tough, easy to grow and low-maintenance. Place goldenrod in an open, sunny part of the garden, shade will make it leggy. Any reasonably well drained soil is sufficient, even hot, poor, dry soils.

Plant goldenrods among asters, gay-feathers and other late-summer-blooming wildflowers. Their arching plumes attract butterflies and contrast beautifully with these companion plants. Alternatively, grow goldenrod as a single specimen, highlighting it against a dark green hedge or a dark fence. When it reaches its flowering peak, cut a few sprays for a striking indoor arrangement, or let the plumes seed and then cut them for dried flower arrangements (see page 61).

If goldenrod becomes leggy or straggly, trim back the stems in June; they will flower by fall as more compact plants. To prevent overcrowding, which encourages the disease rust, and to keep the flowers prolific, divide the plants every two or three years, discarding the old center (see page 39).

Showy goldenrod is a prairie wildflower that grows easily from seed, blooming the second year.

IRIS

Iris species

Named after the Greek goddess of the rainbow, irises come in many colors. Even a single type may range from white and buff to blue and reddish purple. Irises are mostly native to moist habitats, although several will grow in dry soils. All the plants shown here spread to form colonies. Use them in a rock garden, woodland garden, border or water garden. The flowers bloom from early spring to early summer; their sword-shaped leaves contrast beautifully with other foliage. Divide iris every three years or so to keep it vigorous and flowering prolifically.

Douglas iris
I. douglasiana
Douglas iris is one of the most adaptable native iris. It thrives in dry soils, in sun or partial shade and in heat too. However, it is a West Coast native and needs to be brought indoors for the winter in areas where temperatures fall below 10° F. Douglas iris blooms as early as February in California coastal gardens. Its flowers range from white and yellow to blue or purple. The stems may grow to just 6 in. or as tall as 2 ft.

Blue flag
I. versicolor
Blue flag is a robust, water-loving iris. It forms dense colonies and flowers on 3-ft. stems. Set it in water if you like, the swollen rhizome just below the water surface, or place it anywhere the soil is always slightly moist. Blue flag flowers for 2 or 3 weeks during May, June or July. It needs a sunny or very lightly shaded site and fertile soil. It is native to parts of the Northeast and Midwest.

Dwarf iris
I. verna
Dwarf iris is a diminutive 6 in. at most, the smallest native iris. Place it in a rock garden; it loves a sunny or partially shaded position with well-drained, sandy soil and regular watering. Native to the Southeast, dwarf iris prefers an acid soil, with a pH of 5 or below. Add plenty of leaf mold to the soil every year, and feed lightly with a fertilizer formulated for acid-loving plants. Its violet-blue to white flowers open in early spring.

Dwarf crested iris
I. cristata

Dwarf crested iris spreads rather slowly, but otherwise makes an excellent ground cover, especially for a sloping site. It is also showy enough to be used for lining a path through a woodland garden or as a specimen in the front of a rock garden or border. Its 4- to 9-in. blue-purple flowers open in April or May. Place this iris from the Southeast in well-drained soil in sun or partial shade. It needs only moderate watering.

Western blue flag
I. missouriensis

Western blue flag is native to moist meadows from Colorado to California. Choose a sunny place for it that is damp at least for the first part of the year; it is drought tolerant after it blooms in early summer. Its large flowers range from pale blue to blue violet; the stems grow to 20 in. Western blue flag tolerates poor soil and heat.

Dividing Irises

First Divide irises every few years, when they become overcrowded, to provide a bountiful source of easily established new plants. In late summer or fall, dig up the mature runners—the thick, swollen stems usually visible at the soil surface. Gently hose the soil off the fibrous roots.

Then Using a sharp knife, cut away 4-in. sections of the rhizome. Each piece should have fibrous roots and a fan of leaves. Trim back the foliage to 6 in. Replant the pieces at least 6 in. apart at the depth of the original plant, the runners above ground and the roots covered with soil. Firm the soil, and water immediately.

JACK-IN-THE-PULPIT
Arisaema triphyllum

This perennial wildflower has an intriguing name and form: The *Jack* is the upright, finger-like part of the flower, called the spadix. The *pulpit* is its hood, or spathe. For greatest effect, plant this small perennial in clusters of five or more and choose a location that highlights it, for example, along a woodland path, in a container, among a rich green backdrop of ferns or at the edge of a pond. Its curious flowers, the hoods often beautifully streaked with maroon or green and white, bloom in late spring and early summer. In late summer or fall, thick clusters of scarlet berries appear on the Jacks.

Jack-in-the-pulpit needs a shady, moist habitat with plenty of decomposed organic material in the soil. A moist woodland is perfect; there it will reach two feet, produce its magnificent berries and multiply.

Jack-in-the-pulpit, *A. triphyllum,* is a choice woodland garden plant, prized for its unusual flower in spring and its brilliant fall berries.

WOODLAND WILDFLOWERS

Bee balm
Bleeding heart
Bunchberry
Columbine
False miterwort
Geranium
Great blue lobelia
Iris
Jack-in-the-pulpit
Lilies
Pasque flower
Phlox
Violet
Virginia bluebells

A WOODLAND GARDEN

Even in a small city yard, a woodland garden can provide seclusion and respite from a hectic schedule. Two or three well-spaced small trees plus a few shrubs or tall wildflowers are sufficient to make an airy, private place where dappled light plays through a canopy of leaves, creating patterns on a rich-smelling woodland floor.

Most woodland wildflowers are spring flowering; species including Jack-in-the-pulpit give soft splashes of color before the leaf canopy provides too much shade. In summer, woodland gardens are typically cool, green places, where variegated shrubs and delicate fern foliage provide the texture and woodland wildflowers such as lilies provide blooms. Berries and changing leaf colors light up the woodland garden in fall.

There are two requirements for a woodland garden: summer shade and year-round moisture. Choose a place that is partially shaded, where, for example, plants receive a few hours of morning sun or filtered light all day. Very few plants will grow in full, dense shade where they receive no direct sunlight.

Natural woodland soils are rich in decomposed organic material. If your soil is poor or only moderately fertile, dig plenty of compost, leaf mold, or manure into the garden two or three weeks before you plant. If you are gardening around established trees, make pockets of rich soil between the roots and avoid changing the soil level; a few extra inches of soil over its roots can kill a mature tree. Let the fallen leaves remain on the woodland floor through the winter to make a nutritious mulch. In early spring remove some of the mulch so that small wildflowers, such as Virginia bluebells and pasque flower, can push through to the surface.

LILY
Lilium species

A west coast native, the leopard lily, *L. pardalinum,* produces up to 15 flowers per stem in early summer. Sometimes the bird- and butterfly-attracting orange flowers have purple or maroon spots.

MAJESTIC TRUMPETS

It's hard to imagine a more personally rewarding conservation project than designing and planting a garden featuring six-foot native lilies that each bear a dozen or more exquisite blossoms. About 20 lilies are native to North America, but because their habitats are disappearing, the wild population is under siege. Growing a few lilies—first checking that they have not been collected from the wild—is a worthy ecological act.

Most lilies are native to the eastern half of the continent, where they grow in wet meadows and open woodlands. Lilies do well in deep, cool soils with plenty of organic material and at least fours a day of direct sun. If you plant them in full sun, mulch the plants in spring with three inches of leaf mold or compost to keep the roots cool.

Although lily roots like an evenly moist soil, the bulbs may rot unless the soil is well drained. Plant the bulbs in fall or very early spring. Work soil amendments into 12 inches of soil and place the bulbs four to six inches below the soil surface. To discourage mice and moles from eating them, leave some large pieces of sharp gravel around the bulbs or line the hole with hardware cloth.

Lilies are glorious almost anywhere in the garden. Plant them in small groups through a flower border. Surround them with equally tall plants such as goldenrod, which will provide them shelter from wind and camouflage the lily leaves when they turn yellow in late summer. The brilliant flowers are also dramatic in front of deep green shrubs and as cut flowers. The fragrant lilies, in particular, make striking container plants.

Canada lily
L. canadense
Canada lily produces up to 20 fragrant blooms on a stem that may reach 5 to 6 ft. It flowers for a few weeks in June and July. Flowers range from yellow to orange. It is native to moist eastern meadows.

Turk's-cap lily
L. superbum
One of the most prolific-blooming lilies, Turk's-cap may produce as many as 50 orange-red flowers on each stem. It flowers in mid summer and grows to 7 ft. Its native range is moist areas of the eastern half of the continent.

Michigan lily
L. michiganense
Michigan lily grows to 5 ft. It blooms in July and August with 2 to 5 flowers per stem. The orange-red petals are so reflexed that their tips meet. This lily is native to the Midwest.

Wood lily
L. philadelphicum
Wood lily has upright flowers, and unlike most lilies, it tolerates dry soil and partial shade. Up to 5 red or orange flowers per 2- or 3-ft. stem open in early to mid summer. Native to open woodlands of the eastern states, it prefers an acid soil.

LUPINE
Lupinus species

Lupine is an understandably popular choice for any style garden. Its dense flower spikes tower above striking foliage; several species are fragrant and can be cut for magnificent indoor arrangements. Annual types self-sow prolifically anywhere there is a well-drained soil in a sunny location. Perennial lupines last only a few years so are best regularly replaced with new plants grown from seed. Unless you choose a moisture-loving type, water lupine only to get it established because overwatering causes mildew. Lupine is a member of the pea family; its seeds form in small green pods. If you start from seed, first soak the seed overnight in warm water to soften the coating. If you buy plants, handle the ball gently because the roots do not like disturbance.

Blue-pod lupine
L. polyphyllus
Broadleaf lupine grows to 5 or 6 ft. and produces long, fragrant flower spikes in May that are excellent as cut flowers. It is more adaptable than many lupines: give it sun or partial shade and a moist soil. This perennial lupine is native to the western states.

Perennial lupine
L. perennis
Native to the East, from Maine to Louisiana, and to Texas, the perennial lupine forms a 2-ft. bush and blooms from May to July. Dry, poor soil suits it best and full sun. It is sometimes called sundial plant, because during the day its leaves swivel to follow the position of the sun.

Arroyo lupine
L. succulentus
The arroyo lupine is a fragrant California annual that bursts into bloom as early as February, often accompanying California poppies. The 8- to 30-in. flower spikes range from purple and rusty red to blue. Arroyo lupine will grow in dry, poor soils and is pollinated by honeybees.

Silvery lupine
L. argenteus
This 18- to 36-in. perennial lupine has silvery green foliage, which makes a group of it quite distinctive in a flower border. Place it in full sun. Its blooming season is June through August. Silvery lupine is native to dry, rocky slopes in the West.

Texas lupine
L. texensis
The deep blue flowers of Texas bluebonnet appear on thousands of miles of roadsides in Texas in April and May. Very tolerant of drought and soil types, this 12- to 24-in. annual thrives in most gardens too, provided it receives moisture in fall and spring.

Sky lupine
L. nanus
This dwarf, fragrant, native California annual grows to 4 to 18 in. Its rich blue flowers are usually speckled with white. Mass sky lupine on a sunny bank with its fellow West Coast natives clarkia and California poppy. They should all be in bloom in late spring. Sky lupine needs moisture in spring.

Whitewhorl lupine
L. densiflorus
One of the 80 or so lupines native to California, the annual whitewhorl lupine flowers from April to June. It does better in a sunny location and grows well in dry or poor soils. It grows to 2½ ft. The flowers may be white, yellow, blue or purple.

53

PASQUE FLOWER
Anemone nuttalliana

SPRING CHARMER

Pasque flowers are high on the list of many wildflower enthusiasts' favorite plants. In early spring, a single clump of pasque flowers, just six inches or so tall, will steal everyone's attention. The pale lavender blue flower cups with gold centers emerge before the leaves, sometimes pushing up through snow. The foliage is whitish green, fernlike, silky. The fruits, feathery clusters of seed like clematis fruits, appear by midsummer and are another greatly admired feature of the pasque flower.

Given that it is such a stunning plant, position pasque flower carefully. It needs a simple, intimate setting to reveal its beauty. A place in a sunny rock garden (see page 63) will do it justice, or at the front of a border as long as its neighbors provide a plain backdrop and not a visual distraction. A particularly dramatic setting would be in a woodland garden (see page 49) below tall deciduous trees (casting only very light shade), with no shrubs or taller perennials to break the contrast in scale. A container of pasque flower placed so that it is visible from the house makes a delightful first signal of spring.

Pasque flower loves sun. It will spread quickly in a well-drained, fertile soil that is moist in late winter and early spring. During summer, when it becomes dormant, it will tolerate drought and heat.

You may find pasque flower labeled under its old name, *Anemone patens,* a European native. Botanists recently recognized that the North American native, *A. nuttalliana,* is a different plant.

The state flower of South Dakota, pasque is native to the prairies, the western mountains and Alaska.

Garden Care

Wildflowers, by definition, need no human intervention to grow and multiply. If you have chosen plants suitable for your garden soil and climate (see page 19), they will need little maintenance.

Spend the most time ensuring new plants will establish well by watering and weeding them regularly. Once the plants are growing vigorously, slowly cut back on the watering of drought-tolerant plants. Follow the recommendations in the plant descriptions, because even though many garden plants grow more abundantly with plenty of water, overwatering some wildflowers kills them. Likewise, many wildflowers need little, if any, feeding if planted in appropriately fertile soil.

Deadhead flowers that have faded by snapping or cutting the stem just below the flower head. Many plants will produce a second set of flowers after deadheading. Stake a top-heavy plant by pushing in a support cane alongside it and loosely tying the stem to the cane with soft twine. If an entire clump becomes unruly, as goldenrod may, place three tall canes around the base and loop the twine from cane to cane.

Think twice before reaching for chemical solutions to pests or diseases. Beneficial insects, which prey on pests and pollinate flowers, will die along with the pests if you apply chemicals. Try removing pests by hand or by rinsing the plants in a soap solution. Remove diseased leaves if only a few leaves are affected. Remember to wash your hands and tools after touching diseased plants so you do not spread the disease.

Spreading a few inches of organic material around growing plants, called *mulching*, suppresses weed seedlings, helps keep the soil moist and provides nutrients as the materials decompose. If you cannot keep on top of the weeding by pulling weeds as they appear, at least be sure to remove them before they set seed.

PENSTEMON
Penstemon species

There is a dizzying choice of penstemons suitable for any sunny, well-drained spot in your garden. More than 200 species of this pretty plant with foxglove-like flowers are native to the United States. The tall herbaceous plants from the East and South thrive in moist borders; the desert and mountain species are perfect for a dry slope or a desert garden. Because all penstemons must have well-drained soil, in heavy soils consider adding a generous shovelful of organic material to the planting hole to prevent plants from rotting. Penstemons are mostly short-lived perennials, lasting three or four years.

Pineleaf penstemon
P. pinifolius
Native to the southwestern deserts, this small, shrubby, evergreen penstemon thrives in a soil without added organic material. It makes a fine rock garden plant, in sun or shade, growing up to 12 in. and flowering in late spring and sporadically through the summer. Water it every 2 weeks to keep the flowers—and hummingbirds—coming.

Rocky Mountain penstemon
P. strictus
Rocky Mountain penstemon forms a loose mat of evergreen foliage from which 2-ft. flower spikes emerge in early summer. It is drought resistant once established, but occasional watering will improve the flowers. Native to the mountains, this penstemon will thrive in a poor soil in sun or partial shade. It is ideal on a dry slope to control erosion. The deep blue flowers are shown here against the bright orange pineleaf penstemon.

Large-flowered beardtongue
P. grandiflorus
Large-flowered beardtongue is native to dry prairies. Plant a dozen or so close together on a sandy slope or in a well-drained border. They grow to 3 ft. in full sun or partial shade and flower in late spring. Large-flowered beardtongue is best replaced every other year, because it loses vigor quickly.

White beardtongue
P. digitalis

A group of 3 or 5 white beardtongues make a majestic display in a border. The flowers are showy and open on 4-ft. stems. Native to the East and South, white beardtongues thrive in sun or partial shade but like fertile, rich soils and moisture, even constant moisture. The foliage dies back in winter. White beardtongue is a longer-lived plant than many penstemons.

DESERT WILDFLOWERS

Blanket flower
California poppy
Clarkia
Coneflower
Evening primrose
Lupine
Penstemon
Sunflower

A DESERT GARDEN

Desert natives are used to dry winds, alkaline soils, extremes of temperature and long droughts. In average gardens a thousand miles away from a desert, most will grow luxuriantly. And there's no shortage of choice: the deserts in the Southwest contain the largest diversity of annual wildflowers in the United States, many of them fragrant and delicate.

A hot, dry bank planted with evening primrose makes a simple desert garden full of fragrance after sunset. Adding one or two boulders, yuccas, cacti, other perennials such as penstemon, grasses, or a mat of annuals will provide striking contrasts in form and texture. For an authentic desert look, leave lots of space around shrubby plants and cacti, and grow a carpet of annuals over everything.

Desert gardens are most beautiful under wide skies and brilliant sunlight. Moist, shady gardens with pale winter sunlight are better planted with woodland natives. Resilient as they are, desert wildflowers quickly rot in a rich, damp soil.

The perfect soil for a desert garden is sandy, very low in organic materials, and fast draining. Regular watering is essential to get even desert natives started. Some will flower more profusely if you keep up the watering; however, most desert natives do not need regular watering once they are established. The perennials have developed ways to endure long droughts, for example, by producing extensive roots that run deep into underlying rocks or by reflecting sunlight from their gray or silver leaves. Desert annuals germinate with the first drops of a cloudburst and quickly produce flowers to ensure their life cycle is complete while moisture lasts. The seeds often have hard cases, keeping them viable for many years if drought makes that necessary.

PHLOX
Phlox species

All but one of the 60 or so kinds of phlox are native to the United States, but it was European plant breeders who launched them as popular garden plants. Phlox are simple to grow. Choose among soft-colored, loose ground covers, pretty mounding plants, and the magnificent tall phlox the English grow in garden borders. Many are deliciously fragrant. Cut back the spent flower stems, and phlox will often produce a second flush of foliage and flowers. Avoid mildew by watering at the base, not overhead, and removing old stems to improve air circulation.

Grow this eastern woodland native perennial, wild sweet William, *P. divaricata*, in moist organic soil and partial sun or shade. Its fragrant blue flowers appear in April.

Creeping phlox
P. stolonifera

Creeping phlox is an eastern woodland perennial. Although it tolerates heat, it does best in shade, in moist soil rich in organic material. It spreads quickly, producing a loose tumble of large, scented flowers, about 8 to 12 in., for a month in midspring. The flowers are lavender, violet or white. To start a new patch, divide after flowering.

Summer phlox
P. paniculata

Summer phlox is the highly fragrant 4- to 6-ft. phlox that graces the back of cottage flower gardens. Its pink, lavender, blue or white flowers last for 2 to 6 weeks in mid to late summer. Plant summer phlox in deep, rich soil, and water it regularly. Divide the clumps in fall, 3 or 4 stems per piece. Summer phlox is native to the eastern half of the continent.

Drummond's phlox
P. drummondii

Drummond's phlox is an annual and easy to grow from seed. If you deadhead the flowers and keep the plant watered, it will bloom from spring until the first frost. A Texas native, this phlox grows well even in poor soil and hot conditions; it needs only full sun and good drainage. The flowers are purple, pink or white, and grow to about 12 to 18 in.

Thick-leaf phlox
P. carolina

Another perennial phlox for a sunny border, thick-leaf phlox grows to 1 to 4 ft. and flowers in late spring and early summer. Like summer phlox, it needs a fertile, organic soil and a sunny or partially sunny position. The flowers are lavender, pink or occasionally white. Thick-leaf phlox is native to the eastern woodlands.

PURPLE CONEFLOWER
Echinacea purpurea

BRISTLY BEAUTY

Purple coneflower is a match for any of the showy hybrid flowers breeders develop for the florist trade. Its stiff, three-foot stems support a bristly mahogany cone ringed by drooping pink-purple petals, a bold, coarse-textured flower that looks equally magnificent in a sunny border or a vase.

Purple coneflowers bloom continuously from June to October. The flowers last many weeks, and cutting the stems at the base encourages the plant to keep sending up more.

Three plants in a sunny border will provide plenty of flowers for the house. Plant them alongside their native prairie companions black-eyed Susan, coreopsis, and butterfly weed; together they will make a beautiful prairie garden that will attract butterflies. The stately form of purple coneflower also makes a striking contrast among billowing mounds of native grasses.

Purple coneflowers are easy to grow in any sunny garden, providing the soil is well drained. In heavy garden soil, work plenty of organic material into the planting hole. A moist, rich soil will produce the tallest stems, but purple coneflowers are extremely adaptable. They tolerate heat, poor soil and even drought once established.

Keep the plants healthy by dividing them every three years. Lift the clumps in fall, and tease apart the sections for replanting, positioning the buds just below the soil surface.

Purple coneflowers act as a magnet for butterflies, including monarchs. Cut, garden-grown coneflowers will last longer than most florist flowers.

USING GARDEN FLOWERS

From even a small wildflower garden, there are usually blooms to spare for use indoors. Pick flowers just before they reach their peak, whether you are gathering flowers for a fresh bouquet or for drying. Carry a bucket containing some water with you. Set the cut ends in the water while you continue gardening.

To make cut flowers last, mix commercial flower food into warm water in a clean vase. Remove foliage from the bottom of the stems and cut the stem diagonally before placing in the water. Change the water every two days (or five days with flower food), trimming the stems each time. Place the vase in a cool place out of direct sunlight and away from ripe fruit or vegetables. Flowers that exude milky sap from the stems—coneflowers, sunflowers, California poppies and clarkias—last longer if you singe the ends over a lighted match before putting them in water.

There are three ways to dry flowers: air-drying them, placing them in silica gel or pressing them (see page 67). To air-dry flowers, you need a cool, dark, well-ventilated room so that they keep their color and dry without rotting. Hang small bunches, four or five stems in a rubber band, upside down from a rack or nail. Spread the stems so the air can circulate among them. Bee balm, gay-feather and goldenrod dry well this way.

Silica gel dries flowers in just two or three days, retaining much of their original color. Place a layer of the granules in an airtight container. Remove all but one inch of the flower stem, and place a six-inch piece of florists' wire into the end of each stem. Lay the flowers in the silica. Carefully brush granules in among the petals and then completely cover them with granules. Seal the container, and leave it for two days.

SHOOTING STAR
Dodecatheon species

CYCLAMEN FAMILY MINIATURES

Shooting stars are small specimen plants: the intriguing pink, reflexed flowers with yellow throats and maroon pointers deserve a prime position in the garden. Cluster them along a path or at the front of a rock garden, somewhere they are bound to be noticed.

Members of the cyclamen and primrose family, shooting stars are native to most areas of the United States, except the Southwest, which is generally too arid for them. Common shooting star, *D. meadia,* blooms in late spring. It is most often seen in open eastern woodlands and prairie meadows. It will grow even in moderately acid soil. Several other native shooting stars grow well in the garden. Western shooting star, *D. clevelandii,* grows a little less tall, to 18 inches, than the eastern one and is a sturdier-looking plant although slower growing. Its early-spring flowers are spicy fragrant. The western shooting star is tender to frost, most suitable for the coastal areas of California.

Shooting stars need a rich organic soil and moisture in spring; the rest of the year they are drought tolerant. After flowering, the plants go dormant until the following spring. If you want to avoid a bare spot, overplant them with a simple, nonaggressive ground cover. Shooting stars grow well in partial shade or full sun.

Common shooting stars sometimes have lilac or white petals instead of pink ones. The leaves form rosettes, often red-tinted. They are plants well worth viewing up close.

A Rock Garden

A rock garden is an exhibition area. Exquisite miniatures that would be lost among other plants at ground level can be dramatically presented on a raised stone ledge or in a crevice between boulders.

Choose and place the rocks carefully. In the garden, mimic the way rocks occur together in the wild. Decide on one type of rock, and gather a range of sizes, including a few large ones so you can sink them deep into the ground for a natural effect, and a selection of shapes—irregular boulders, flat ledges, shards and pebbles.

Once you are satisfied that the arrangement of the rocks looks natural, fill the pockets between the rocks with a soil that will suit each plant. Rock garden purists grow only alpine natives and use a fast-draining soil mix that is mostly coarse sand. Many of the wildflowers in this book will grow in a sunny rock garden with a sandy soil. If you want to include plants that need a rich soil, such as shooting stars, simply replace most of the sandy soil with garden compost, leaf mold or decomposed manure in that one spot of the rock garden.

A shady spot is a perfect site for a rock garden of prize woodland plants and ferns. Use a rich soil and keep it damp, according to the plants' needs.

Draw up a list of small plants for a small rock garden; large ones will seem out of scale. Select a mixture of creeping, mounding and upright plants. Consider adding one or two dwarf evergreen shrubs and some miniature bulbs for visual interest throughout the seasons. Plant a few delicate annuals for a fast splash of color while the perennials become established. Finish your rock garden with a mulch of gravel or pine needles if you have made a shady woodland rock garden.

ROCK WILDFLOWERS

Bellflower
Bleeding heart
California poppy
Columbine
Dwarf iris
Evening primrose
Geranium
Lupine
Pasque flower
Penstemon
Shooting star
Violet

SUNFLOWER
Helianthus species

The native sunflowers have smaller flower heads than the modern giant hybrids but a far more glorious history. Indigenous throughout the Americas, they were worshipped by the Incas as a symbol of the sun. Spanish explorers took their seed back to Europe, and early settlers thought sunflowers could ward off malaria. Today, gardeners plant sunflowers mostly for their brilliant color in late summer. Growing up to eight feet, they are particularly effective highlighted along a fence or at the back of a sunny border. Birds adore sunflower seeds; cover the heads if you want to collect some for sowing.

Maximilian sunflower, *H. maximiliani,* is a long-lived adaptable perennial. It will grow well in most garden conditions, including partial shade, poor and dry soils and heat, making it suitable for prairie gardens (see page 41) and desert gardens (see page 57).

Collecting Seed

First Collect no more than 10 percent of the seeds from wild plants. This method is similar for all seed-bearing flowers, including sunflowers and blanket flowers (shown here).

Then Tap the seed head or container to see if the seeds are loose. If not, protect your supply by tying a paper bag over the head.

Third Once the seeds are ripe, collect them in an envelope or paper bag. Some need special cold treatments or flower only several years after sowing.

Fourth Air-dry the seeds in a cool room, basement or garage where the humidity is low. Drying them outdoors will attract birds and rodents.

Next After 4 days, separate the seeds. Shake or beat them free, using a rolling pin if necessary to crack open the seed pod.

Last Mark envelopes to identify various seeds. Then sow the seeds immediately (see page 27) or store them in an airtight container in the refrigerator.

VIOLET
Viola species

Violets are especially fine perennials for a wild-flower garden. Place them in containers so that you can appreciate their delicate petal coloring up close: downy yellow violet has purplish brown veins, Canada violet petals are purple on the back. They are also effective massed in a woodland garden or a sunny rock garden (some do well in a moist, rich soil, others on an arid, gravelly slope). The heart-shaped leaves make an attractive ground cover once the spring blooms fade. Many violets self-sow into thick clumps that you can divide in fall.

Downy yellow violet
V. pubescens
Downy yellow violet seeks out shady areas with moist, rich soils. It is a native of the eastern woodlands and Midwest. Choose a sheltered spot for this violet, keep it uniformly moist and mulch around it in spring and fall.

Canada violet
V. canadensis
Canada violet grows in moist, rich, woodland soils from Alaska to Alabama, the Southwest, and Oregon. It does well in partial shade and with a spring and fall organic mulch. Place it among other plants to disguise its declining foliage in summer.

Labrador violet
V. labradorica
Labrador violet is a fast-spreading, tiny variety, just 2 or 3 in. tall. Plant it between stepping stones or at the front of a rock garden. It grows wild in the North and Northeast and needs shade and moisture.

Pressing Flowers

First Choose wildflowers from your garden that provide beautiful material for crafts to make a pretty greeting card or bookmark. Many flowers will press well, especially ones with thin petals and flat centers, such as violets, evening primroses, and California poppies as well as leaves and grasses.

Third Place a 1-in. stack of newspapers on top of one book. Tape a piece of white paper or a smooth white paper towel to the newspaper to keep the newspaper ink from staining your flowers. Set the flowers face down on the white paper, making sure that they don't touch one another and that the petals aren't folded.

Then Pick flowers that have just opened and are unblemished. Snip off some leaves, too. If the flowers have thick stems, discard the stems. Gather two heavy books, newspaper and white paper or paper towels. Alternatively, use a flower pressing kit available from many garden centers.

Last Press the centers flat. Cover with another sheet of white paper and more newspaper. Put the other book on top. Check your flowers after 2 weeks. Seal your arrangement with clear adhesive paper.

Native to the eastern half of the continent, bird's foot violet, *V. pedata,* thrives anywhere there is dry, poor soil with good drainage. A sunny rock garden is a perfect spot.

67

Virginia Bluebells

Mertensia virginica

Spring Ephemeral

Virginia bluebells are one of the very easiest wildflowers to grow in the eastern United States. If you have a piece of ground that stays moist in spring, they will thrive there. Plant them with daffodils or crocuses for a very showy spring flower garden or scatter them throughout a woodland garden (see page 49).

Virginia bluebells are called ephemerals because they are short-lived: they send up new leaves, flower, disperse seeds and die back within just a few months. Come summer, they are gone, so it is best to organize a second show, perhaps ferns or fringed bleeding heart planted in among the bluebells.

Native to the eastern woodlands, where the soil is damp and rich with decomposed organic materials, Virginia bluebells must have moisture in late winter and spring, their active growing season. However, once they go dormant in mid summer, they will tolerate dryness. If your soil is not naturally rich in organic material, add manure, decayed leaf mold or compost to the soil when you plant and mulch the area each spring. Enriching the soil also improves drainage and protects plants from rotting at the crown, a problem only in boggy soils. Virginia bluebells grow well in sun or shade.

Once it is established, this wildflower multiplies rapidly. It seeds prolifically and also spreads by producing new buds on a vigorous root system. To start a new patch, dig up a mature clump just as the plants go dormant and gently pry away portions of the brown roots, checking that you have a bud or two in each portion (see page 39).

Virginia bluebells make a reliable spring ground cover of nodding pink buds that unfold into blue flowers.

WATER LILY
Nymphaea odorata

A single native lily in a small pond or tub will release wafts of sweet fragrance through the summer months and turn even the tiniest patio into an elegant space. Water lilies need sun all day and still water. The native water lily is a perennial, but if the water in the tub is likely to freeze, remove the lily in late fall and store it in damp newspaper in a cool basement until spring. Unfortunately still water will attract mosquitos to your garden, so place a few gold-fish or mosquito fish, available from a pet store, in your lily pond to eliminate the problem.

The fragrant blossoms of the only water lily native to North America open in the morning and close at noon. They reach 6 in. across, held above 9- to 12-in. pads. This lily and the naturally occurring pale pink and dwarf white varieties grow wild in eastern wetlands.

Making a Water Lily Tub

First In spring, partially fill a wide, shallow pot with clay soil that has little, if any, organic material. Purchase aquatic compost or take soil from the garden if it is suitable. Add to the soil 1 tab of fertilizer formulated for water lilies or 2 tabs of fertilizer for trees and shrubs. Water the soil thoroughly to remove as much air as possible.

Third Gather a tub or any other watertight container that is at least 18 in. deep, bricks and a full watering can. Avoid using a redwood container, because it may discolor the water. Place the brick in the tub, and put the pot on top. Start to fill the tub, pouring gently, so that the soil does not muddy the water. Fill until the pot is covered with 4 in. of water.

Then Trim away the large, mature foliage from the lily rhizome so that once it is planted the leaves do not float it to the surface. Also trim away any damaged roots. Place the water lily horizontally on the soil, and cover it with 2 in. of pea gravel to anchor it in the pot. Water the pot thoroughly.

Last Raise the water level as the lily grows, eventually removing the brick. Through the summer, push a new fertilizer tab into the pot each month. Unfortunately, despite your best gardening efforts, many water lilies will not bloom until the second year. In extreme cold-winter regions, remove the lily rhizome in late fall and store it indoors until spring.

VIEWING WILDFLOWERS

Wildflower gardening is a popular activity across the nation. Most states have a native plant society or wildflower preservation society that organizes lectures and tours to regional wildflower gardens and natural habitats. The National Wildflower Research Center (2600 FM 973 North, Austin, TX 78725), founded in 1982 with the support of Lady Bird Johnson, produces an information package on growing regional wildflowers for almost every state. Its *Wildflower Handbook* lists sources of wildflower seeds and plants in all 50 states along with propagation techniques and wildflower organizations and gardens to visit.

The Menzie's Native Plant Garden in San Francisco's Golden Gate Park is a fine example of a regional wildflower research site as well as an excellent place to view California natives.

GARDENS TO VISIT

ALABAMA Birmingham Botanical Garden, Birmingham, 205 879-1227. **ARIZONA** Arizona-Sonora Desert Museum, Tucson, 602 883-2702; Boyce Thompson Southwestern Arboretum, Superior, 602 689-2811; Desert Botanical Garden, Phoenix 602 941-1225. **CALIFORNIA** Rancho Santa Ana Botanic Garden, Claremont, 909 625-8767; East Bay Regional Botanic Garden, Berkeley, 510 841-8732; Santa Barbara Botanic Garden, Santa Barbara, 805 682-4726; Strybing Arboretum Society of Golden Gate Park, San Francisco, 415 661-1316; University of California Botanical Garden, Berkeley, 510 642-3343. **COLORADO** Denver Botanic Garden, Denver, 303 331-4010. **CONNECTICUT** Connecticut Arboretum, New London, 203 439-2144. **DISTRICT OF COLUMBIA** Kenilworth Aquatic Gardens, Washington, 202 426-6905. **DELAWARE** Winterthur Museum and Gardens, Winterthur, 800 448-3883. **GEORGIA** Callaway Gardens, Pine Mountain, 706 663-2281. **ILLINOIS** Chicago Botanic Garden, Glencoe, 708 835-5440; Morton Arboretum, Lisle, 708 719-2465. **INDIANA** Hayes Regional Arboretum, Richmond, 317 962-3745. **MASSACHUSETTS** Arnold Arboretum, Jamaica Plain, 617 524-1718; Garden in the Woods, Framingham, 508 877-6574. **MICHIGAN** Fernwood Botanic Garden, Niles, 616 695-6491; University of Michigan Matthaei Botanical Gardens, Ann Arbor, 313 998-7061. **MINNESOTA** Minnesota Landscape Arboretum, Chanhassen, 612 443-2460. **NEW JERSEY** Leonard J. Buck Gardens, Far Hills, 908 234-2677. **NEW YORK** Bayard Cutting Arboretum, Oakdale, 516 581-1002; New York Botanical Garden, Bronx, 718 817-8700. **NORTH CAROLINA** North Carolina Botanical Garden, Chapel Hill, 919 962-0522. **OHIO** Holden Arboretum, Kirtland, 216 946-4400. **OREGON** Berry Botanic Garden, Portland, 503 636-4112. **PENNSYLVANIA** Bowman's Hill Wildflower Preserve, Washington Crossing, 215 862-2924; Brandywine River Conservancy's Wild Flower and Native Plant Garden, Chadds Ford, 610 388-2700; Longwood Gardens, Kennett Square, 610 388-6741. **TEXAS** San Antonio Botanical Garden, San Antonio, 210 821-5115. **VERMONT** Vermont Wildflower Farm, Charlotte, 802 425-3500. **WISCONSIN** University of Wisconsin Arboretum, Madison, 608 263-7888.

WILDFLOWER REFERENCE CHART

	PLANT TYPE			CLIMATE ZONE	GROW FROM		BLOOMS			LIGHT			SOIL	
	Annual	Perennial	Biennial		Seed	Division	Spring	Summer	Fall	Sun	Partial Shade	Shade	Dry	Moist
Aster														
New England aster		•		3–8		•		•	•	•				•
Bee balm		•		4–9		•		•		•	•			•
Bellflower		•		2–9		•		•		•			•	•
Black-eyed Susan		•		3–9	•			•	•	•			•	•
Blanket flower	•	•		2–9	•		•	•	•	•			•	
Bleeding heart														
Dutchman's breeches		•		3–7		•	•				•	•		•
Fringed bleeding heart		•		3–8		•	•	•	•		•			•
Western bleeding heart		•		4–8		•	•	•			•	•		•
Bunchberry		•		1–6		•		•		•	•			•
Butterfly weed		•		3–10	•			•		•			•	
California poppy	•	•		All	•		•	•		•			•	•
Cardinal flower														
Cardinal flower		•		2–9		•		•		•	•			•
Great blue lobelia		•		4–9				•		•	•			•
Clarkia	•			All	•		•	•		•			•	•
Columbine														
Blue columbine		•		2–8	•		•	•		•	•			
Golden columbine		•		3–9	•		•	•		•	•		•	•
Wild columbine		•		3–8	•		•	•		•	•		•	•
Coneflower														
Coneflower		•		4–10	•			•		•			•	
Prairie coneflower		•		6–8	•			•		•			•	
Coralbells														
Coralbells		•		4–9	•	•	•	•		•	•		•	•
Alumroot		•		5–8		•	•	•		•	•		•	•

	PLANT TYPE			CLIMATE ZONE	GROW FROM		BLOOMS			LIGHT			SOIL	
	Annual	Perennial	Biennial		Seed	Division	Spring	Summer	Fall	Sun	Partial Shade	Shade	Dry	Moist
Coralbells (*continued*)														
Small-flowered alumroot		•		7–10	•		•	•		•	•		•	•
Coreopsis														
Lance-leaved coreopsis		•		3–9	•	•		•		•			•	•
Plains coreopsis	•			All	•			•		•			•	•
Evening primrose														
Desert evening primrose		•		8–10	•		•	•		•			•	
Hooker's evening primrose			•	4–10	•			•	•	•			•	•
Missouri evening primrose		•		4–8	•		•	•		•			•	
Ozark sundrops		•		5–8	•	•		•		•			•	•
Showy evening primrose		•		5–9		•	•	•		•			•	
Tufted evening primrose		•		4–9	•			•		•			•	
White evening primrose		•		7–9	•			•		•			•	
False miterwort			•	3–9		•	•	•			•			•
Gay-feathers		•		4–9		•		•	•	•			•	•
Geranium														
Wild geranium		•		4–8		•	•				•			•
Goldenrod		•		2–8	•			•	•	•			•	•
Iris														
Blue flag		•		2–7		•		•		•	•			•
Douglas iris		•		9–10	•	•				•	•		•	•
Dwarf iris		•		6–9	•	•					•			•
Dwarf crested iris		•		3–9	•	•				•	•			•
Western blue flag		•		3–6	•	•	•	•		•				•
Jack-in-the-pulpit		•		4–9		•	•				•	•		•
Lily														
Canada lily		•		4–9		•		•		•	•			•

	Annual	Perennial	Biennial	CLIMATE ZONE	Seed	Division	Spring	Summer	Fall	Sun	Partial Shade	Shade	Dry	Moist
Lily (*continued*)														
Leopard lily		•		4–9		•	•	•		•	•			•
Michigan lily		•		5–8		•		•		•	•			•
Turk's-cap lily		•		4–9		•		•		•	•			•
Wood lily		•		4–7		•		•		•			•	
Lupine														
Arroyo lupine	•			All	•		•			•			•	
Blue-pod lupine		•		7–10	•		•	•		•	•		•	
Perennial lupine		•				•		•		•			•	•
Silvery lupine		•		3–6	•			•		•			•	
Sky lupine	•			All	•		•			•			•	
Texas lupine	•			All		•	•			•			•	•
Whitewhorl lupine	•			All	•					•			•	
Pasque flower		•		1–7		•	•			•			•	•
Penstemon														
Large-flowered penstemon		•	•	3–5	•	•		•		•	•		•	
Pineleaf penstemon		•		5–10		•		•		•	•	•	•	•
Rocky Mtn. penstemon		•		4–10		•		•		•	•	•	•	
White beardtongue		•		3–9		•		•		•	•			•
Phlox														
Creeping phlox		•		2–9		•	•				•	•		•
Drummond's phlox	•			All	•		•	•	•	•			•	•
Summer phlox		•		4–8		•		•	•	•	•			•
Thick-leaf phlox		•		3–9		•	•	•		•	•			•
Wild sweet William		•		3–9		•	•				•	•		•

	PLANT TYPE			CLIMATE ZONE	GROW FROM		BLOOMS			LIGHT				SOIL	
	Annual	Perennial	Biennial		Seed	Division	Spring	Summer	Fall	Sun	Partial Shade	Shade		Dry	Moist
Purple coneflower		•		3–8		•		•	•	•				•	•
Shooting star															
Common shooting star		•		4–8		•	•			•	•				•
Western shooting star		•		8–10		•	•			•	•				•
Sunflower															
Maximilian sunflower		•		5–10	•			•	•	•	•			•	•
Violet															
Bird's foot violet		•		4–9		•	•			•				•	
Canada violet		•		3–8		•	•				•	•			•
Downy yellow violet		•		3–7		•	•				•	•			•
Labrador violet		•		All		•	•				•				•
Virginia bluebells		•		3–9		•	•			•	•				•
Water lily		•		All		•		•		•					•

INDEX

A NOTE FROM NK LAWN & GARDEN CO.

For more than 100 years, since its founding in Minneapolis, Minnesota, NK Lawn & Garden has provided gardeners with the finest quality seed and other garden products.

We doubt that our leaders, Jesse E. Northrup and Preston King, would recognize their seed company today, but gardeners everywhere in the United States still rely on NK Lawn & Garden's knowledge and experience at planting time.

We are pleased to be able to share this practical experience with you through this ongoing series of easy-to-use gardening books.

Here you'll find hundreds of years of gardening experience distilled into easy-to-understand text and step-by-step pictures. Every popular gardening subject is included.

As you use the information in these books, we hope you'll also try our lawn and garden products. They're available at your local garden retailer.

There's nothing more satisfying than a successful, beautiful garden. There's something special about the color of blooming flowers and the flavor of home-grown garden vegetables.

We understand how special you feel about growing things—and NK Lawn & Garden feels the same way, too. After all, we've been a friend to gardeners everywhere since 1884.